UNSOLVED MYSTERIES

THE BERMUDA TRIANGLE

BY ORLIN RICHARD

ABOUT THE AUTHOR

Orlin Richard is a children's book author and editor from Fargo, North Dakota. He has written and edited books about sports, science, and history for elementary and middle-grade students. In his spare time he likes to ponder the mysteries of the world.

Published by The Child's World®
1980 Lookout Drive • Mankato, MN 56003-1705
800-599-READ • www.childsworld.com

ACKNOWLEDGMENTS
The Child's World®: Mary Berendes, Publishing Director
Red Line Editorial: Editorial direction
The Design Lab: Design
Amnet: Production

DESIGN ELEMENT: Shutterstock Images

PHOTOGRAPHS ©: Witold Krasowski/Hemera/Thinkstock, cover; Nicholas Rjabow/Shutterstock Images, 5; Bettmann/Corbis, 7, 11; AP Images, 13; Shutterstock Images, 15; Beth Swanson/Shutterstock Images, 16; iStock-photo, 18; Stockbyte/Thinkstock, 20; Shi Yali/Shutterstock Images, 23

ISBN 9781634070706
LCCN 2014959770

Printed in the United States of America
Mankato, MN
July, 2015
PA02266

TABLE OF CONTENTS

MYSTERY OF FLIGHT 19

It was 2:10 p.m. on December 5, 1945. Five
U.S. Navy planes took off on a training flight.
They departed from the U.S. Naval Air Station in
Fort Lauderdale, Florida.

Lieutenant Charles Carroll Taylor had
command of Flight 19. He would fly one of the
planes. There were four other pilots. Nine crew
members were also on the planes.

It was 67°F (19°C) outside. There were light
clouds. It was good weather for a flight. The

The Flight 19 planes were similar to this torpedo bomber.

planes had just refueled. They could fly for five and a half hours.

The plan was to fly to the Bahamas. The planes were torpedo bombers. The pilots would practice dropping their torpedoes. Then they would return to Fort Lauderdale. Taylor thought the flight would take two hours.

The flight plan seemed simple. But things soon went wrong. Taylor picked up his radio at about 3:45 p.m.

He reached a Navy officer in Fort Lauderdale. Taylor said he was lost. The officer asked for his compass readings. But Taylor said that his compasses were broken. He thought he was over the Florida Keys. Others in Fort Lauderdale tried to help. A team attempted to guide the planes home.

It was getting later. The weather was getting worse. Soon, Taylor lost radio contact with the Fort Lauderdale team. Hours passed. The planes did not return.

The Navy launched a massive search effort. But searchers found no trace of the crew. One rescue plane was also lost after sending a message that its crew had begun their flight. The airmen and five planes from Flight 19 were never seen again. The rescue plane and its crew were also never found. They had been lost in the Bermuda Triangle.

Understanding the Bermuda Triangle

The Bermuda Triangle is in the Atlantic Ocean. It spans about 500,000 square miles (1,300,000 sq km). The three points of the Triangle are Puerto Rico, the Bahamas, and

A poster shows a yacht that went missing in the Bermuda Triangle in 1974.

7

Miami, Florida. More than 20 airplanes have disappeared there. At least 50 ships have been lost in the area.

Ships and planes have gone missing in the Bermuda Triangle since 1840. People disagree about what causes the strange events. Some blame bad weather. Others think **supernatural** forces are to blame.

Navy officials tried to explain what happened to Flight 19. They thought Taylor was incorrect about his location. He had said he was over the Florida Keys. But perhaps he was really above the Bahamas. This mistake could have caused him to fly off course. The planes would have run out of fuel. The crew might have made an emergency water landing. They would have had little chance of survival.

Some did not accept the Navy's explanation. Flight conditions had been good. Taylor was an experienced pilot. Could he really have gotten lost? Other questions remained, too. Why did the compasses stop working? Why was no wreckage found? And what happened to the missing rescue plane?

Many tried to solve the mystery. Some said aliens lived in the Bermuda Triangle. Perhaps they captured the planes. Others said that sea creatures attacked the crew. A few thought the crew had traveled in time. These explanations might seem unlikely. But Flight 19 was a strange case. No one knows for sure what happened to its planes and crew.

Are strange forces at work in the Bermuda Triangle? Some people think so. Scientists are still looking for answers.

CHAPTER TWO

THE HISTORY OF THE BERMUDA TRIANGLE

Strange things have happened in the Bermuda Triangle for a long time. Christopher Columbus sailed there in 1492. He was the first European in the area. Columbus reported seeing strange lights. He also had problems with his compass. It did not point north.

Columbus's crew survived their trip through the Bermuda Triangle. But some ships' crews did not. In 1918, a U.S. Navy cargo ship disappeared. The U.S.S. *Cyclops* departed from the island of Barbados. It was due to reach Baltimore,

The U.S.S. *Cyclops disappeared in 1918.*

Maryland, five days later. The ship had a crew of more than 300 people. Many were skilled sailors.

The *Cyclops* never reached Maryland. The ship was lost in the Bermuda Triangle. The crew was never found. It was the Navy's largest loss of life outside of a battle. Some think the ship sank. It may have been caught in a storm. But there is no proof. The ship's fate remains a mystery.

After the loss of Flight 19, the legend of the Bermuda Triangle grew. More mysteries followed. A plane left San Juan, Puerto Rico, for Miami in 1948. During the flight, **air traffic controllers** lost contact with the pilot. The plane and its 29 passengers vanished.

Experts studied reports about the plane. It may have had electrical problems. The plane probably crashed. But no wreckage was ever found.

Naming the Triangle

The Bermuda Triangle got its name in 1964. Reporter Vincent Gaddis named the area in his article "The Deadly Bermuda Triangle." The area has other names, too. Some people call it the Devil's Triangle. Other names include the Port of Missing Ships and the Twilight Zone.

Disappearances continued after Gaddis's article. One happened in 1965. A U.S. Air Force Reserve plane departed from Florida. The plane had a highly experienced crew. The flight was headed for the Bahamas. It did not arrive. No one knows why. The pilot never sent a distress call. Most likely, the plane crashed. But experts had no proof. There were no survivors. Teams searched for traces of the plane. They found only a few strips of metal.

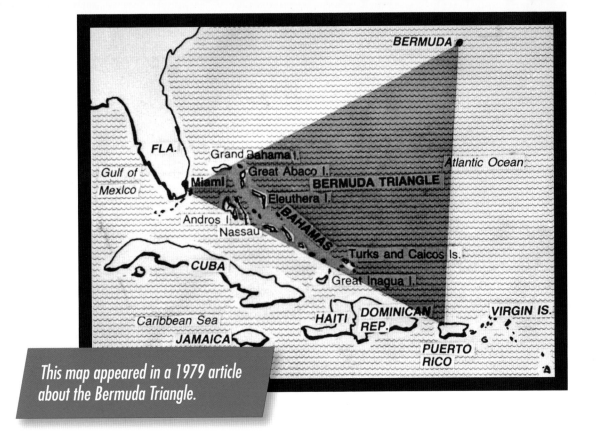

This map appeared in a 1979 article about the Bermuda Triangle.

Today, crashes in the Bermuda Triangle are rare. Few disappearances occur. But they still do happen. In 2008, a small plane departed from the Dominican Republic. The pilot was flying to the Bahamas. One hour later, he contacted air officials. He was lost in the Bermuda Triangle. The plane disappeared from radar screens. Officials lost contact with the pilot. The plane disappeared with 12 people aboard. They were never found.

Experts still are not sure how this plane was lost. Many other cases are also unsolved. People have a variety of **theories**. Soon, we may know if one of them is true.

CHAPTER THREE

EXPLANATIONS OF THE BERMUDA TRIANGLE

Many explanations of the Bermuda Triangle are supernatural. They involve aliens and strange fog. Other theories are scientific. They involve weather conditions or human errors.

Aliens and Atlantis

Some people link the Bermuda Triangle to aliens. They say aliens **abduct** crews. Others wonder about alien technology. They think it affects planes or ships. This would explain compass problems in the area.

This picture shows an artist's idea of what Atlantis might look like today.

Another idea is that the ruins of Atlantis are in the Bermuda Triangle. Atlantis was a **mythical** island. People wrote about it many years ago. Atlantis may never have existed. But some say it sank into the ocean. According to legends, Atlantis had powerful tools. Some think this technology has caused ships to disappear. Or perhaps aliens live in Atlantis. **Portals** in Atlantis could lead to other worlds.

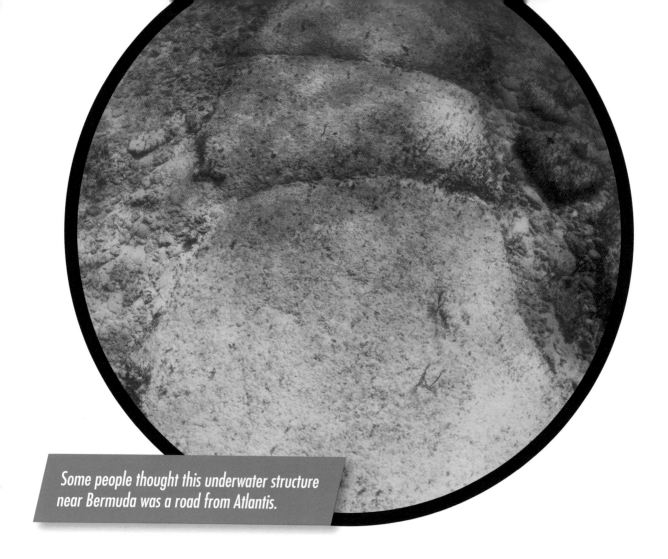

Some people thought this underwater structure near Bermuda was a road from Atlantis.

In 1968, divers found an underwater structure in the Bahamas. It looked like a road. This structure supported the idea of Atlantis. Some said it was from the ancient city. But most experts thought the "road" was a natural formation. Similar structures were found near Cuba in 2001. Some thought the structures were from a sunken city. Scientists **debunked** this idea.

Mysterious Fog

A strange fog is another explanation. Bruce Gernon owned a small plane. In 1970, he was flying to Bimini, a district in the Bahamas. Gernon saw a cloud in the distance. It had strange round edges.

According to Gernon, the cloud expanded. It formed a tunnel. He flew through it. His compass did not work in the fog.

When the fog cleared, Gernon was over Miami. The pilot was stunned. He thought it was impossible to travel to Miami so quickly. Gernon said he had traveled through time. He wrote a book about his flight. Gernon also spoke about other lost planes in the Bermuda Triangle. He thought they had traveled to another time, too.

Many people doubt Gernon's story. But some believe it. One other pilot reported similar clouds. He called it a time storm.

The Agonic Line

Gernon said his compass did not work in the Bermuda Triangle. Others have reported the same problem. Some navigators have offered explanations. Compass magnets do not point to the geographic North Pole. They point to the magnetic North Pole. Sailors know about the difference between the poles. They calculate the difference when they navigate.

The agonic line is an imaginary line. It goes around Earth's surface. The line marks an area where magnetic

Compasses act strangely in the Bermuda Triangle.

north and geographic north lie in the same direction. This line was once in the Bermuda Triangle. Some say that compasses do not work on the agonic line. Others think the agonic line confuses sailors, since it changes their calculations. As a result, they could make navigation errors.

The agonic line moves. It is now in the Gulf of Mexico. But some say the agonic line caused past disappearances.

Scientific Explanations

Many scientists have other theories. Weather is one important factor. Human error also causes many wrecks. People get lost at sea. Planes run out of fuel.

Weather causes most air and water disasters around the world. The Bermuda Triangle often has sudden storms. Storms may form too quickly for people to avoid them. Crafts can disappear without a record of storms in the area.

Waterspouts can wreck ships. The Bermuda Triangle also has a lot of **seismic activity**. This can cause giant waves called rogue waves. Rogue waves rise up suddenly. They can be more than 50 feet (15 m) tall. These waves can sink ships.

Mighty currents run through the Triangle. One powerful current is the Gulf Stream. It can move at more than 5 miles

Waterspouts are tornadoes that form over water.

(8 km) per hour. That is enough to knock ships off course. Ships can get lost as a result. Some never find land. Skilled sailors know how to adjust for the current. But other sailors may not. Currents also cause some violent weather.

Often, **amateur** pilots travel in the Bermuda Triangle. Their inexperience may cause wrecks. Amateur pilots are often less skilled than professional pilots. They may struggle to steer through harsh weather.

Many routes cross the Bermuda Triangle. Planes and ships pass through it every day. Most have no problems. Common errors can account for most of the wrecks. But many are still unexplained. Scientists have theories about what might have happened. But they do not yet have the answers. Until they do, the Bermuda Triangle will stay a mystery.

Glossary

abduct (ab-DUKT) To abduct someone is to take the person away. Some people think aliens abduct crews in the Bermuda Triangle.

air traffic controllers (AIR TRAF-ik kun-TROL-erz) Air traffic controllers are workers who keep track of planes. Pilots communicate with air traffic controllers during flights.

amateur (AM-uh-chur) An amateur is someone who does something, such as flying a plane, for fun but not for work. The amateur pilot only flew on weekends.

debunked (dee-BUHNKT) Something that has been debunked has been proved false. Many Bermuda Triangle theories have been debunked.

mythical (MITH-i-kuhl) Something that is mythical is not real. Atlantis is considered mythical because there is no proof it existed.

portals (POR-tulz) Portals are openings, such as doors, that lead somewhere else. Some think that portals exist in the Bermuda Triangle, leading to other worlds.

seismic activity (SIZE-mik ak-TIV-uh-tee) The seismic activity of an area is what happens on Earth's surface because of earthquakes or other underground vibrations. Seismic activity may contribute to weather patterns in the Bermuda Triangle.

supernatural (soo-pur-NACH-ur-uhl) Something that cannot be explained by science is supernatural. Many believe supernatural forces exist in the Bermuda Triangle.

theories (THEE-reez) Theories are possible explanations for events. There are many theories about the Bermuda Triangle, but few can be proved.

waterspouts (WAW-tur-spowts) Waterspouts are tornadoes that form over water and carry water many feet into the air. Waterspouts can sink ships.

To Learn More

BOOKS

Hawkins, John. *Atlantis and Other Lost Worlds*. New York: PowerKids Press, 2012.

Stone, Adam. *The Bermuda Triangle*. Minneapolis: Bellwether Media, 2011.

Walker, Kathryn. *Mysteries of the Bermuda Triangle*. New York: Crabtree, 2009.

WEB SITES

Visit our Web site for links about the Bermuda Triangle: **childsworld.com/links**

Note to Parents, Teachers, and Librarians: We routinely verify our Web links to make sure they are safe and active sites. So encourage your readers to check them out!

Index